Acknowledgements are due to the editors of the following magazine in which some of these poems first appeared:
Aabye's Baby; The Affectionate Punch; Airelings; Apostrophe; The Brobdingnagian Times (Ireland); *The California Quarterly* (US); *The Coal City Review* (US); *Current Accounts; Dandelion; Fire; Green's Magazine* (Canada); *Heart Throb; Interactions; Iota; The Journal; The Journal of Contemporary Anglo-Scandinavian Poetry; Lateral Moves; Poetry Monthly; The People's Poetry; Poetry Now; New Hope International; Other Poetry; Paris/Atlantic* (France); *Psychopoetica; Pulsar; Raw Edge; Rustic Rub; Sepia; Staple New Writing; Target; Various Artists.*

Some of these poems, or early versions of them, also appeared in the following pamphlets: *First Communion* (Norfolk: Michael Green); *Funny Old Game* (Norfolk: Michael Green); *The Right Suggestion* (Redditch: Flarestack Press).

'Catch a Falling Tortoise,' 'Mr Bray's Toupee,' 'Circles,' and 'Artist' were all prize-winners in the annual Ottakars/Faber and Faber poetry competition.

Paul McDonald is Senior Lecturer in Creative and Professional Writing at the University of Wolverhampton. He is the author of several books of literary criticism and two novels. His hobbies include sudoku and supporting Walsall Football Club. He uses the former to take his mind off the latter.

Contents

For Pam

Catch a Falling Tortoise

Hide and Seek

Kyle wasn't like the other kids.
He'd say, *Give me 30 seconds*
and you'll never find me.
We could have, if we'd tried.

He'd search for dead things
on the railway tracks
and put them in his pocket.
That's how it started.
Later he was fined for
doing something to a cat.
Experts intervened.

Most kids didn't like him.
He'd tell us heaven was invented, and love.
Somehow we knew he knew.
I can see him now. Hiding.

Mr Bray's Toupee

Head of Year Mr (Toupee) Bray asked
what in blue blazes we were doing when
he caught us swapping spit beside
the science block. We didn't have an answer
so we were sent our separate ways: you to
double maths; me to find a way to skive P.E.
We were young as dawn sunlight in a rabbit's eye –
and randy too, eager for each other like
the separated halves of something shameless.
And it wasn't just the Head of Year who
witnessed our embrace. The blushing Walsall sky
always framed us in our passion: at the bus stop,
at the park, or in our favourite field. The tall blades
of grass would rise around us like bamboo.
Could a hundred pales of water have untangled us
or kept us from our chocolate box of buttons,
zips and clasps? More chance of Mr Bray relinquishing
his toupee. We were blind, deaf and daft
with the thrill of each other. Even as I write
I can feel our French kisses. We checked our eyes
were closed by opening them. Our love thinned
and fell away in time, of course, and there was
no point hanging on once it had gone.
Like Mr Bray's toupee it couldn't grow.
Was it just a surface lustre that impressed us?
It felt real enough to fool us for a while.

Greetings from Vegas

Hotel great. I'm in room
twelve thousand four hundred and six.
It has a mirrored ceiling and I spend the
mornings waving at myself. Good view of the Strip.
Paris can be seen from here (I kid you not, buddy).
You can fit a jumbo jet in the Jacuzzi and,
downstairs in the lobby, have your photo taken
with a randy marmoset. He wears leather trousers
and a tartan tam-o'-shanter (that's not a lyric, buddy,
it's the truth).
They've Sinatra's hair on show, and Liberace's truss.
And things are cheap, like the bumper sign I bought:
DON'T HONK AT ME WHILE I'M RELOADING.
Went up to the Stratosphere. Nice view.
They've a UFO emporium. It sells
'missing time' detectors and things that bleep
if you begin to float.
I bought one and it went off in the night. Twice.

Artist

Remember that day in Attingham Park?
All afternoon you were twenty yards behind,
photographing flowers and curious fungi:
alien terrains of *Meripilus Giganteus*.

I tracked my silhouette along the river,
identifying pines as Scots
(or maybe Monterey);
you snipered through the undergrowth

and caught the day in crosshairs.
That's what artists do: startle mice with light,
turn grass blades to bamboo.
It would have been just Shropshire

without your point-of-view:
but for these pictures on my lap
the trees would mask the wood.
Now I see the sap.

Circles

I have to take their word that I'm a polar bear.
I wouldn't know. All I do is walk around in circles.
Round and round I go. Perhaps I'm a goldfish.
There have been whispers of the arctic but
I only see this cage, and eyes
behind the humming wire. It's not so bad.

The keepers do their best to keep me sane.
My compound has a pool and its feeds of fish.
Plus I have my circles. Round and round and round
I shoulder my enclosure walls, chase my rear.
At least I'm not a camel: all they do
is sleep. The public get the hump but I cheer them up.

They like to watch my circling for a while.
It takes a dozen laps before they move
on to the chimps. They tire because I never do.
Round and round I go, tracing steps. I know how
many footfalls to a lap; heartbeats. There's rhythm
in my circles, and form: I'm the snake who eats its tail.

I'd be happy but for THEM (the vets that is).
It worries them my walking round and round.
They are squares who don't like circles:
they think I'm off my nut! Whatever next?
They'll be asking me to abdicate my throne,
or telling me a cage is not a home.

Catch a Falling Tortoise

Few things are more sickening
than the crack or clack that
shell would make on impact with
the concrete. Treading on a
cockroach doesn't match it.
Grotesque in flight, a tortoise falls
to earth like a frozen turkey might

or a terracotta pot with contents
so unspeakable no one wants to see.
Everyone is somewhere
and I was there: right place and time
to save the weary dignity of something
seldom looked at (unless it's
polished-up to back a hairbrush).

With such presence and such
languid eyes who could let a tortoise
hit the unforgiving ground?
Heavy as a house-brick it
completed my cupped palms like
something built to need me.
It slapped into my grasp with a

slick and easy *thwick*, delicious
in its substance like a well-struck
cricket ball pouched beside
the boundary rope. There's nothing
much to match it in the satisfaction stakes.
I recommend you catch one
next time you see one falling from the sky.

The Murder of Joe Orton

The silences were Pinteresque between
the knocks at number 25 Noel Road.
The chauffeur shuffled in the hall,
caught glimpses through the letterbox:
the blood, the dodo egg of
Kenneth's head. Soon the police

will shoulder down the door and hear the
clock strike twelve, see the midday sun
light up the dark stains on the lino.
Games of silly buggers often end in
tears, or with someone at the corner
of a bed contemplating sticky hands.

Whoever authored this demise failed to
add the comic edge it needs. It's too dark
as it stands; too true. Truths are always
better sampled second-hand, or filtered through
the eye of someone quick to spot the beauty
in absurdity and, thus, in everything.

Slug

You were weird the day you
Stroked me with that slug.
I didn't understand,
But now I do:
You liked it.
The furrow in my skin,
My cringe against its stardust trail
Like shrinking from the snow.
You said, *Imagine it's*
A mermaid's tongue.
Imagine.
The word SLUG slimed
Across my back.
The licked script.

A Warning

Your cat had been with you for eighteen years
when its ninth life ended; I'd been with you for ten.
We were wary of each other from the start:
I of his chill, sleek shivers, he of my claim on you.
His eyes would drink me, measure by measure.
I can see him now, shapeless and black,
a rattlesnake crouching within. I could sense his
secret knowledge as I watched him stalk,
or stretch, his hindquarters up, his tail a scorpion's
crescent curve. He'd passed a human
hundred when he died and you sobbed on
my shoulder. Mine was a rival's triumph but,
as I stroked your weeping head, all I could
think of was him – his fur electric beneath
my palm: a reminder, perhaps. Or a warning.

The Crab Hunters

Oranges leaded lines baited
with raw fish, stripped white
to the flesh, tumble from the quay.
Beneath the retreating waves the

quarry move on articulate twigs,
feeling with nutcracker fingers
for morsels in the murk.
Periodically lines are raised for

inspection – the heavy ones spooled in,
twenty feet to the top. Often more
than one crab has seized the bait.
As they are air-lifted from safety

they clutch their piece of sushi like a
cigarette between chopsticks.
It's a pincers grip of grim tenacity
that persists till the children shake

them into buckets. Occasionally one
plops back in the tide, saved by a
slackened clasp. Rarer still, crabs
will clatter onto the quay-side

like terra cotta pasties. Then – free
to turn their lateral, spider-rapid
two-step – they scatter the shrieking hunters
who shy, scared of their own supper.

Z Car

My dad's bought a second-hand car –
his last.
His driving days are almost done
he says.
My mother will be chuffed:
no more pools of oil to mark the drive
and underscore his absence.
For fifty years his cars have come and gone:
an A to Z of sumps to feed the stain.
I cherish its resistance
when she scrubs at it.
Indelible and tacky black
it darkens like a slice of night,
and deepens.
It's history:
the chaos that will shape itself
in time.
Before the shadow of the Z car's gone
for good, I'll put my palm-print in its slime.

Ancient Light

Asking the waitress to dance was
probably a mistake. There are
many to be made with your shorts
around your shoes. Did you
notice she was sixty, or
were you too preoccupied with
spaces in between your thoughts?
It took a heavy tip to keep the
taxi-driver sweet, and hours to
get you off the swings and past
the flower-beds. Twice around the
ornamental lake and you were weeping.
You'd lost your watch, and youth,
your tax and MOT were due,
and stars were nothing more than ancient light.
Things aren't what they used to be, you told us.
We sympathized but couldn't disagree
as the chilly, pin-prick light
peaked weakly through the colander of night.

Your Kind

You started in the Bowery:
a burglar, a bouncer, a lad who buys and sells
and stands in smoky corners.
You were born for Uncle Sam with

a smile that opened safes,
a hand that conjured halos out of hats –
your own at least.
Americans have always loved your kind:

your waistcoat made of panda-hide,
your legendary wink.
You were admired the way
a shark is, or a bullet wound.

I once saw you perform: the devil danced
behind your eyes. You kissed a snake's head
for a bet, sucked its mouth to yours
and kept it there, long after you had won.

It's a Funny Old Game

It's a winter night at the football;
the floodlights clean the air.
You're here too in your duffle coat
and Chanel No. 5. You are yawning
as I shout about the man free in
midfield and wonder if our centre-half
is blind. The crowd is a cataract
that you don't seem to see,
slumped down in your plastic seat,
content to watch the patterns that our
breath makes in the air. Are you

wondering why you're here amid these
points you cannot see the point of?
I'm wondering too. I ask if number nine
plays for the Brownies or the Guides,
and inform him, just in case he doesn't
know, that football is a game for men
with skill he sadly lacks. Your hood is up
and you're peering from your dugout when,
suddenly, the crowd is on its feet. You alone
are sitting. When I tell you that we've
missed an open goal you're not surprised.

Death of a Sunflower

In May you denied the slugs so
that by September you could surprise us
with all ten feet of your
wrist-thick stem, green as a gooseberry.
Jack couldn't have climbed
you in a month of Sundays.
The colour of Little Richard's shirt
your bad taste bloom upset our neighbours.
You rubbed them the wrong way with
your yellow yawn and self-celebratory
stare levelled unblinking at the sun.
Where did you learn to be so forthright?
You were born out of place in
Birmingham: you belonged in California,
or in King Kong's buttonhole.
Not here, where next-doors-kids' pellets
could pierce your honest heart.

Victoriana Day

Fractured half-moon spectacles are stacked
for sale in cabinets by boxes long-since
void of snuff. Rusty cut-throat razors have lost
their edge but gain a certain glamour
beside the swords and Boar War bayonets.
It's Victoriana Day. The Town Hall's packed

with foxing prints and yellowed letters stamped
with penny reds and, sometimes, blacks.
Collectors hypnotise themselves with fob-watch
after fob-watch, checking dates and listening
for the purest tick. They've been wound for
the occasion like the clocks that kept the hours

when the working days were longer, like the summers.
Everything's for sale and has a price. The shelves
and tables groan beneath accumulated history.
The past is being pecked away, packaged up and
sold down aisles of teddy bears, faded maps and
irons the weight of anvils. China kings and queens

are keeping court with chamber pots. They are
embarrassed by their cracks but have to face the
market even as they mourn their days of purpose.
It's Victoriana Day and the blushes on the faces
of the Toby Jugs are beaming like they never have before:
the past is a commodity and punters are queuing at the door.

The Swimmer

I know a man who swims alone at the
public baths. He never looks for
company and seldom meets an eye but
seeks the pool at times few others do.
You can find him on cup final afternoons

and weekday winter mornings,
never in the summer or when the kids
are not at school. He's happy when
its empty and he alone steps out
to print the tiles. The patient

gallons hum in the echoing quiet and the
lengths stretch before him, uneaten.
He loves his isolation as he kicks off the
side, heaving oscillations to the pool's
still quarters. He is at the bull's-eye

of all his activity. He never counts the
lengths that vanish in his wake but swims
an hour or two, or until disturbed
by others. Dolphins to his lonely shark,
people cramp, clutter and retard his

linear up and down. He knows how many
breaststrokes it takes to reach the other end.
The same will bring him back to
where he started. He likes this simple logic;
he needs to turn it over in his mind.

Thinking of Easter

Do you remember that bird we had in our
chimney, injured and trapped behind the
gas-fire? We couldn't get at it and so
for days we had to listen while it bustled
and flapped. Like watching cruelty on the
news, what could we do? If not for the fire
it would have burst from the flue with a
thunderclap of soot, the living room alive
with commotion. But instead we heard its
claws needling the brick, aborted
flights for the teasing light. The T.V.
was impossible and you lost your appetite.
Each morning for a week we hoped it would
be dead but it just kept tapping an S.O.S.,
fainter and fainter, making us sick.
When at last it stopped I tried to joke:
perhaps like the Count of Monte Cristo
it pecked out through a tunnel,
grain by grain. Later I caught you at the
chimney breast. I knew you were checking
the plaster. You were looking for cracks and
signs of beak, hoping, and thinking of Easter.

Greetings from Athens

Athens is Athens. Traffic in your face.
My worry beads are worthless. On Sophokleos Street
Christos, or his brother, owns a bar.
He has girls for fifty euros, boys for thirty five.
Transvestites too. Men loiter like hyenas.

At distance almost everything is fine,
even *here*: from the top of Lykavitos
or Philopappos. Socrates died there
in a cave I couldn't find. Nice view of Piraeus,
though, and the blue Aegean.
A single cup of hemlock and I'll never leave.

Buildwas Abbey

Buildwas Abbey's broken ribs
are no surprise to Shropshire.
Time has conquered silence
and bird-calls mock the ruined walls.
Monks no longer search their sleeves
for elbows, breathe illicit whispers.
The end was in the air even as they winced
at echoes of their footsteps.
Endings always are.
The world of noise is bigger
than the world of hush.
Buildwas winds seem to blow
much louder since they left;
crows increase the clamour of their caw.

Saddle-maker

It starts with a vision and a frame,
sprung by pulling webbing tight along the length.
He drum-stretches hide to make a seat,
stroking out creases like a man who lays a carpet.
He sows like a surgeon suturing skin,
pulling threads through wax
to hitch his stitches fast, to charm the flax.
And he hammers tacks: *snap, snap* and *snap* –
bites of lead below the cantle base.
He takes his time with knots,
garrottes them to the spot to keep his vision whole.
Wizards can't untie them.
Saddles have beauty only saddle-makers' see,
and leather speaks. It squeaks, breathes and sweats,
sliming fingers with its tallow.
He can't forget it's flesh.
Their shallows and their depths
convey the rightness of their form.
No need for horses: this art is art.

Dragon's Teeth

The Star Ferry takes you
to the action:
the island that reflects
an iron sky in mirrored walls.
Soon it won't be safe.
The Filipino maids agree
and spend their morning off
trying not to stare at clouds.
The dragon's breath, the heaped and sour
image of its growl, stifles chatter.
Here, where the summer liquefies,
they sell counsel in their crackers:
beware the dragon's teeth
and you'll live to see its tail.

Snake Temple

Temple Snakes hang from eaves,
lean as monkeys' tails,
or drape around the altar, claiming it.
No one tries to count them:
tails are heads and heads are tails.
No one can evict them:
they slither into knots
humans can't untie,
and rear erect like swan's necks
whispering hisses.
Witness their devotions and
Temple Snakes loiter in the mind.
Their gossip mentions you.

Richard

Richard smells of loneliness.
No one likes to be down-wind of him,
or the flares he bought from Oxfam in 1993.
You can find him on his knees beside the flats,
listening to the tarmac.
This doesn't cause a stir:
the local kids see stranger things these days.
Mothers steer their prams around him;
dogs don't take an interest in his scent,
or the esoteric wavelength to which he's tuned.
All about him people fill their days.
They seldom think of him
and he never thinks of them
as the planet hums against his ear.
He alone is bothered by its heartbeat.

Dancing Lesson, 1979

I was dancing at a nightclub
when I pissed a drunken thug off.
I was a ponce and a pansy so he thought
he'd drop-the-nut.

A table took my fall as the breaking glasses
shrieked for me to sober up.
I grew up too, suddenly a man thanks to him:
the guy who taught me not to dance.

He dissolved into a dry-ice fog that lingers.
I search the shadows for him still.
My tea-leaves and the mirror.
Beneath the snare of my chair.

Castaway

He doesn't think it's worth it.
The price he gets for lambs
is nothing short of theft.
And who's around to

help him with the feed?
He's been slogging here
for years, and for what?
A shoebox full of bills.

Sometimes he dreams he's dead.
Last night he dreamt
he was a castaway living in a hut of leaves.
Now he's at his breakfast.

He strains to see his fields
but the window is a mirror.
He turns his gaze away
then back. He needs a shave.

Better Off Dead

If she'd heard you say
what I've heard you
say then she wouldn't
have said that. But then

she's daft as a felt hat.
Dafter come to think of it.
The woman is a gossip and
a shit. Of course it is her

life and she has a right not
to care. But you'd think
she'd be responsible.
She'd be better off dead

and so would the rest
of us. And I'll tell you
this much: if I see her
again I won't look at her.

Enough

We are walking
by that lake,
the one we
nearly broke our
necks to reach.

Remember?

Water measures
the height of reeds,
minutes stretch
like albumen strings.

You remember.

But the words
we spoke are gone.
All that remains is
an empty page,
watermarked through
with an image of us.

It's enough.

My Mate Dave Said to Me Yesterday

Listen Mac, Tracey's just
fifteen and boys already
stare at her with eyes that make
the blank walls blush (or should).
I'm her father for fuck's sake
and I'll have their balls on
cocktail sticks with squares of
cheese and ham. What is it
with the kids these days?
They're randier than Errol Flynn
on oysters. She'll end up in the
blushing mother's club with me in nick
for cutting off the father's dangly bits.
I have Lolita for a daughter.
Corks pop out of bottles when
she passes by; cuckoos spring from clocks.
And she leads them on! She won't listen
to me, Mac, and I'm an adult after all,
twice her fucking age. You'd think
she'd give me more respect.

The Farmhouse Window

The farmhouse window glows with
a buttery light; the silver moon
swings high between the treetops.
While she irons he cleans his gun.

He asks her for more oil; he asks
for another piece of cloth.
So many years they've dwelt here like
a pair of doves, darkness smothering

woods and the distant sea.
Nothing comes between them and they
sleep like stones at night beneath the
quilt she made with careful fingers.

They smile at talk of seasons turned
to dust. They smile to see themselves
repeated in the darkened panes:
no need to hide themselves with curtains.

Priceless

I sit and watch
a scene made
precious by
the window frame.
You move beneath
a yellow moon.
It's round tonight,

a wheel of light
that clarifies
your footsteps
as you near.
You'll be priceless
by the time you
reach my door.

Human

Carlton wore his white collarless shirt
this morning in the newsagent.
He bought some fags and *Exchange and Mart.*
Being stupid makes us human,
Mr Kumar said, referring
to the headline of the *Daily Mail.*
Carlton smiled. *Being human makes us stupid,*
he replied, pocketing his smokes.
I don't think Mr Kumar saw the difference.
Cartlon's shirt was nicely
washed and ironed; it matched
his straight-cut jeans. As he left he drew
a circle round a saxophone
and ticked a double-breasted suit.

Pollock

Someone's had a fit
in the slaughterhouse of oils
where action fought direction, and won.
All deals are off with gravity:
men who court the moment
know the magic of inverted effervescence,
and screaming shreds of light
with no beginning and no end
have the logic of a Dali sky
that rains the lucid spectrum of its bow.

God in a Duffel-Bag

My old mate Andy has found God.
I suppose he must have looked.
I don't know where he found him.
Up a tree; beneath the bed? Now he carries
God around everywhere he goes.

He pushes God before him in a pram;
climbs the stairs with God slung across his shoulder.
Sometimes I think that God would like a break.
To stretch His legs, perhaps; relieve himself.
Andy disagrees. He needs to be reminded

of the happiness he's found in God.
God's OK I guess – like a pantomime, perhaps,
or a plate of fudge. Both can make you happy.
But God can make you *happy happy happy*,
is what Andy says. You just need to take

Him everywhere. This doesn't seem
much fun for God: fancy being stuck with
Andy all the time. One night they joined us
in the pub. Andy had Him in his duffel-bag.
God wanted out I think – to play the fruit machines

perhaps, or read graffiti in the ladies loo.
A pub's no place for prisoners after all. Andy kept
his duffel corded tight across the top but talked
of God and God and God until his beer went flat.
When we see Andy now we say God's name.

Flower

Whirlpools of whisky-air.
Terror air.
For fifty miles that boy has
held a flower in a box.
He sweats while he waits
for the explosion.
We all sweat.
The purple-suited priest,
the two-year-old who's cut his final tooth,
and me.
Some of us have knotted veins, and hatred.
All of us are geckos
in the shadow of a hawk.
Pious folk would worry at my thoughts
as I watch his face.
His sweat.
That flower will kill us all.

Light

You are floating at my mouth:
the womb-clutch touch
that turns you to a reed, you said,

seaweed slack in current.
There are eddies in this sex-lake:
tongue stirred gyres to spin you.

Knot me to your fingers
as you hover, helium-light,
an eyelash height from earth.

Permafrost

Our garden is a charcoal sketch of winter.
You're hard-eyed like the frozen pond
and still, snapshot morning.
The apple tree's a witch's broom;
a garden trowel trapped in soil
is welded to the rock-sod like Excalibur.

I'd tilt the earth for summers that could melt you.
You thought my flame could thaw a pearl,
a wilderness of permafrost: I let you down.
Apologies solidify in air as you walk away;
grass blades crack beneath your feet like spines.

Unnoticed

The barmaid at that nightclub
seemed impressed.
She wrote her number down for
me on a soggy beer receipt.
My wit was dynamite,
my tongue was touch-paper.
The hot air swelled to meet me
as I walked with easy rhythm.
What a club it was! My eyebeams
shone around it like spotlights,
making stars of girls.
They'd wave and laugh,
I'd wave and laugh right back.
But everything was other than it
seemed. Next day I blamed the lager.
I phoned the barmaid's number
and it wasn't hers: it was a
sewage works in Coventry.
Christ-on-skates it rankles.
But there you go. Important things
float by us unnoticed half the time:
Ghosts and clouds and time and truth.
I'm going back again tonight.

The Watcher

R's wife is po-faced. When we go
out in a group she never drinks.
She sits there with an orange juice, aloof.
She's like a poodle. The more we
drink the more she seems to harden:
from stone to steel to diamond. She ruins the
night for R who feels he's being looked
at by his mother. Why does she bother coming?
Whenever there's a party we debate her.
Will she come or not? She always does.
She sits there with her handbag on her lap.

One night we had a beer fight. R's wife
disapproved. She told us if we didn't stop
she'd leave. A dozen drinks flew at her:
lager, bitter, whisky, wine. She sat there
soaked in disbelief. She fished a slice of
lemon from her blouse and stormed into
the grievous night. We thought we'd seen
the last of her, but no. She was out again
next time, thunder in her eyes. I think she
comes to watch us waste our lives.
They leak away with laughter while
she observes and bides her time. Her day is nigh.

Delmore Schwartz on a Park Bench, 1961

Sitting in the park among the pigeons, an
old man of forty seven. His jacket buttons
make a row of eights across his paunch.
His shoes, too warn to tread another
step, have lately only taken him in circles;
now he tries to rest. Elsewhere, old
friends are throwing parties to which he's
not invited: paranoia's tiresome, Modernism's
had its day and no one needs a wino who speaks
ninety words a minute. His needle mind has little
more to do but still it does too much.
It ponders Joyce and Pound but ignores the
smouldering cigarette about to burn his fingers.
He'd like to leave *The Wake* alone but Shem and Shaun
still shimmer in his thoughts: their strange
conspiracies, their brogue, one third English,
two thirds a dream of words. He should have
been a plumber or a carpenter, not a shadow chaser
contemplating shadows of himself.

Sahara

We travelled on the coast road south
from Souse, through Sfax and on.
We made the most of Gabe`s with its
market-garden greenery and cooling-warmth,
like tea. The temperature was rising as we
crossed the plain of Arad where khaki
peaks and gulches provoke a silent sky.
Matmata is a land of molten cheese
where Berbers shade in caves and bury
secrets in the sand. From here the
desert beckons: a universe of couscous
and corrugated air. We breathe its whisky peace:
no summer thunder here; nothing much beyond
the boiled sun and brittle moon. We do not
search for scorpions as tourists often do.
The stinging day's enough for us.
We've come this far to contemplate the
parched grain of the desert. The brutal blaze.

Sorry

You told me you were fine when I phoned
but an image haunted me:
the withered you I'd struggled not to see.
Everyone had gone, leaving you
to search the polished floors,
the blank plaster walls,
for fading hieroglyphics.
Or think. Or crouch inside
the belly of the afternoon
with my electric voice:
Great. I'm pleased. Goodbye.
While our backs were turned
something breached whatever
kept the worst at bay.
I should have joined the fight.
That's bad. I'm sad. How can I put it right?

How Was Your Day?

What have I done with my time
besides eat that pack of
macaroons you warned me not
to touch? Nothing much.
I've been looking at a slice
of sky deciding on which Christian
name I like the sound of least.
If this counts as activity
then I've been occupied.
Oh, I watched a documentary
you might have quite enjoyed:
'Deafness and the Under 35s.'
I SAY I WATCHED A DOCUMENTARY
YOU MIGHT HA – oh, never mind.
I forgot I'm not amusing.
I'm as funny as an arthritic thumb
caught between a hammer and a tack.
And how was your day, darling?
Did you spend the hours
counting smiles? Did you eat
your tuna salad with the plastic fork
provided or use a metal
one from home? By ignoring
me I guess you think I'll go away.
(Darren, by the way, don't ask me why)

Aunty Maud

There are three things I don't
like about life and two of them
involve my nephew Keith.
And the third? Don't ask about
the third when I've a trillion things
to do. I've to re-seed the seed
bed, see to the pepper plant and
think – just think mind you – about
changing the bandage on the
cat's carbuncle. Oh, and by
the way, there are serpents in the
privet hedge, long and sleek
and knotted like sausages.

You've Done a Million Things

You demonstrate the proper way to
eat a passion fruit and I ignore you
even though I watch. *I was rubbing*
rhubarb on my head when you
arrived, I say, *I hear it cures baldness.*

You've done a million things: had dinner
with the manager of Boots, bought some
dungarees with a daisy on the bib
etcetera.
I've been staring at my naked wrists
mostly.

You talk for half-an-hour, your words
becoming pictures in the air,
and hanging.

Then you claim you need to feed
your nephew's salamander
and leave.
I'm trying turnips next, I just have time to say
as you
and your dungarees
desert my day.

Towpath

They walk at the side of the canal
as lovers often do here. It's
early evening and the sky's reflection
fades in the darkening water.

They've been speaking lately of
marriage, now they are silent.
The words they've been using are
somebody else's. They walk on.

The canal carves the distance,
its towpath straight as a Roman road,
or an answer. From now on they
sense that life will just happen.

Underfoot the gravel eats nuts, content.
Among the reeds a fish floats.
Following horses long since vanished,
they continue. They are deepening a furrow.

Nothing Else

He sees her sitting in the glow of the
kitchen window. She is smoking,
staring at the dark like it was art,
or something you might cool your face in.
He keeps his eye on her as he creeps towards
his garden shed. Here are all the
things she cannot see: his spade,
the lamp without a shade, and the
creosoted walls that soak up light.
He turns a spider's web around his thumb.
He likes the way it clings. He likes the way it
shrinks to meet his flesh. Nothing seems to
match the simple, secret things.

This Space

This space was made for us,
its shape completes us
like a mattress does, or water.

Its walls have ears that
check the shallows of our breath.

We make noises that it likes
and understands. It wants to
keep them fast beneath its hat.
Private.

We all belong in rooms like ours.
They swell and shrink to meet us;
they take us round the world, keep
us up among the clouds.

Soon a breeze will make the door vibrate.
Familiar shiver. It makes us shiver
too like a summer shower does,
or the right suggestion.

Responsibility

I think of all the aunts
I should have kissed when
I was young. They past
away in time like the countless
birthday flowers never sent.
Now I'm as old as they were.

I knew age would make its
claim on me and sure enough
it has: it lifts me like the FA cup,
but no one cheers. I'd love
to make a speech to set the record
straight. Or find someone to listen.

Re: Your Request for a Reference

I am more than happy to provide
a reference for Susan. She has studied
a number of my modules during her time
as an undergraduate. She is a conscientious
and able student. Her academic work is
of a good standard and she has received
a number of well-deserved 2i grades.
Susan is a regular attendee and she generally
has something useful to say in seminar
discussions. She exhibits a delightful
enthusiasm for literature. If given the
opportunity I have little doubt that Susan
has the determination and ability to succeed.
I once saw her mime the spectacle of
an epileptic fit. Though her performance was
a little unseemly, she was very convincing.

In Tiananmen Square

A million souls can stand here while Moa
shines out across it like the moon
and comrades stare with tourists
at the man who challenged art, and grass.
There are children flying kites today,
pulling hard against the sky.
A yellow wind blows in from the Gobi
to chase the birds away and make the
old folks hide their heads in bags.
We photograph Qianmen Gate
and men who scream through
narrow eyes. We watch the bikes
float by; we listen to the traffic
growl and thunder. I think of tanks,
faded grins, and imagine
waking-up to find the circle squared.
The people have no English,
we have no Mandarin, so all we do is
wander to each compass point.
All they do is stare and sometimes fail to smile.

On a Train in Finland

Travelling north
towards an
endless day
and distance.
From Helsinki
through to
Tampere the
sky stays
parabolic,
the pine trees
crowd around
half frozen lakes.
I'd be fit for life if
I could stay
for however
long it takes
to make me
brilliant white.
Finland.
A freezing sigh,
a note that almost
shatters in the
gaping cold
as I hurtle
over glass,
chasing possibilities
promised by
the midnight sun.

A Poem for Charles Bukowski

You can know him,
peel back the layers
of his skin, page by page.

There's no point sipping beer,
no point sniffing wine.
He'll tell you that
they're both for gulping
down. Your head goes back,
your eyes close tight
like navels: swallow it
before it swallows you.

He'll tell you this if you
can bear his breath, if you
can peel through to his onion heart.
It smells of flophouse sweat but the
truth is there, squatting
like an ape: it picks its nose;
it curls its bottom lip.

He'll teach you how to
fight and lose; he'll teach you
how to wear a face of plums.

Los Angeles is warm and wide
and nothing seems to hide there
except him. He's looked for
like a mermaid; he's wondered at.
But you can find him if you choose
to soak him up, drink him down.
He's tangible. Prod him with a stick.

Big Roy

The primaries have shaken
off their subtler hues and
The Waiting Blonde is drained
of her third dimension.
This is big Roy's world
where detail is replaced
by screens too close for comfort.

Victories over diffidence are
always the hardest fought and there
are images too bold to bear,
too cruel to shield us with
a compromise. Big Roy can hold
these in his eye, unflinching.
His eye is steady like the
O in pop or the spot that
dots the i in Lichtenstein;
his eye is steady when
the layers have been peeled
and the shadow of deceit
is shunned and a bigger lie revealed.

Picasso's Portrait of Gertrude Stein

The man who painted you was the only
other genius that Alice Tolkas knew.
As you posed amid the clutter at Montmartre,
Fernande read you *La Fontaine*,
index finger high above her head.
You breathed the fumes of oil; he swore in Spanish,
smoothed his thinning hair.
When he saw you that first time he came to dine
his bootblack eyes swallowed you in gulps.
He glimpsed the angle in your rounded
cheek, the sadness in the laugh that
rubbed its back against the priceless walls.
Soon there'd be no need to pose.
He charmed life into your lines while you
were home with musty books and ink.
Too late to hide from eyes you saw were true,
and the only other genius that Alice Tolkas knew.

The End

Walking
in a fading day
emerging from a
dream
spending
time
taking
time
hanging on to
time
I'm dawdling
behind myself
and
must
moderate
my pace
as I near
the end
I fear
the end
I must
p(os)t
pOnet(h)
e
d(r)eAdFuleN
(d)
.